THE ESCAPE

FUTUREPOEM BOOKS
NEW YORK CITY
2003

THE ESCAPE

JO ANN WASSERMAN

FIRST EDITION | FIRST PRINTING | DECEMBER 2003

This edition first published in paperback by Futurepoem books
Futurepoem books, P.O. Box 34, New York, NY 10014
www.futurepoem.com
Editor: Dan Machlin
2002/2003 Guest Editors: Anselm Berrigan, Brenda Coultas, Laird Hunt

Design: Anthony Monahan (am@anthonymonahan.com)
Photographs © Jo Ann Wasserman

Text set in Scala.
Printed in the United States of America on acid-free paper.

This book was made possible, in part, by grants from Fractured Atlas, the
New York Community Trust and the New York State Council on the Arts
Literature Program.

Distributed to the trade by Small Press Distribution, Berkeley, California
Toll-free number (U.S. only): 800.869.7553
Bay area/International: 510.524.1668
orders@spdbooks.org
www.spdbooks.org

Thanks to the following for their scrutiny of, and support with, early drafts of this book:
Susan Angle, Christopher Barickman, J. W. Butler, David Cameron, Tom & Angelica Clark, Brenda
Coultas, Tom D'Angelo, Kathleen Fraser, Gloria Frym, Sandra Gillespie, John Larson, Gillian McCain,
Tish Parmeley, Sarah Palermo, Judith Schiller, Eleni Sikelianos, Rebecca Skeele, Dean Wasserman
and John Yau.

Thanks also to the Fund for Poetry for assistance during the writing of these poems.

Gratitude to Dan Machlin, Futurepoem, and its 2002 editorial panel.

Some of these poems have appeared previously in *The East Village* and *can we have our ball back?*

Quote on p. 87 from Walter Benjamin (translation Harry Zohn, edited with an introduction by
Hannah Arendt), *Illuminations* (New York: Schoken Books, 1968).

Quote on p. 111 from Marcel Proust (translation C.K. Scott Moncrieff, Terrence Kilmartin),
Remembrance of Things Past (New York: Knopf, 1982).

for Tom and Angelica Clark

&

in memory of my mother, Nancy (1933–1986)

PART ONE

PART TWO

PART THREE

PART ONE

The notes begin with the words *motherhood, fortune, providence, the stars* and then *depression, waves of corruption & rot. here is the false Italy.*

These are typical of a notation I make. Encoded immediately. As I write or rewrite, I fail to understand my own writing and then think something out of that amnesia. This is how I came to think many incorrect things.

But I have been to Italy. The actual Italy. There is a notebook full of notes written in Italy. I was there with Susan for a reason that had to do with Switzerland. The real Switzerland. The Switzerland which meant, at that time, that a woman named Dorothy had been treated very badly in every country except Switzerland.

NOVEMBER 15, 1990: *We are in Florence. A man gave us tickets to a disco as soon as we arrived. On the train sat next to a guy who talked and talked, first in Italian then in English mostly about how Newark, NJ, is a real "shit-hole."*

What man?

The one who gave us the tickets I mean. I have no memory of him. I went to Italy so that my boyfriend would break up with me and, at first, he didn't. I had to continue traveling for months. To Italy, Switzerland, France, and England. France was about a woman named "Madame" who could barely walk the three flights up to an apartment she wished to rent to us and I would say, "Madame, if you need to stop . . . " or "Madame, may we hang the blanket out to dry?" That kind of thing until I had a cough so bad that I, too, could no longer go up and down the three flights of stairs and she just said, "Excuse me, American." I ate giant bowls of corn flakes and made cowboy coffee.

In England I called my boyfriend from a pay phone on the street in Bath. I was suddenly unsure about wanting us to break up. I had been thinking about how he would wake up in the middle of the night wanting to cook a lobster dinner. This had grown to seem endearing. Or perhaps I was afraid of being left alone in England forever. Of having that cough forever. Which did actually happen. The cough part. It was January. I called him standing at a phone on the street. I returned home from London and he had painted everything in the apartment black, including the telephone.

None of that is written.

Instead I wrote about meeting a man in Italy who looked like a monk but who was really an architect from New York City. He took us to the ruins of a fortress but never explained his strange, monk-like hair cut. He had a roommate named Lars on the Via di Città in Siena. He invited us for dinner and made a stew of kumquats, grapes, and persimmons and told me, "You are somehow Japanese." It was about that time, actually, at that dinner, that I began to believe in Armageddon. Meaning a big showdown. This feeling is well-documented in a notebook.

There is something that I write to myself frequently. I write that I need to remember to write. I write this over and over again in numerous notebooks. I write that I need to be in mental control. That I need to write more. I am always writing that.

Also I write down when things remind me of my mother. Anything round, soft, sad, expensive, pink, of or like a lake or waterfront, or disaster related. This type of writing is obscure and often illegible: *tin & isabelle saved a ti palm-sized [kitten]. tell J. about Bill's monster soap.* I read these things which I have written at an earlier time and do not recall who Isabelle or Bill or J. are. I read them and understand that I am trying to write a message sounded out in the body.

There are these two things I write about more than anything else:

Writing.
My mother.

But I have only written the writing part. I have not written about you. I write about writing about places. Being in airplanes. Sitting on trains. Falling asleep in the passenger seat.

So you will know what the whole world looks like.

OCTOBER 1997: *On a train. There is an ice cream called Turkey Hill. And men running for office. I see street corners at early evening. Red neon and a the smell of meat cooking. Somewhere on this train there is meat being cooked. Because the heat won't quit. I am somewhere in northern New York State. There are Value Meals and newlyweds. And a loud boy named Vince whose mother has a huge head of permed hair. Some things never "come back." To be a hairstyle or describe the whole world is a hard job.*

I wrote something in a notebook dated August 18, 1987, about being on my way to New York City and thankful for a moment to trim my fingernails. I was going to

Baltimore later in the day and hoped that the thing would go off without a hitch. The thing certainly did not go without a hitch. The thing was hitches all the way down. This was mostly because I was taking pills. The white kind. The thing, as I recall, ended up as a near-death experience, but early in the day I had been hopeful. I write that I have been off pills for three days. I am somewhat hopeful but can not shake a feeling that I have squandered everything in my life. I write that I wish I could try something aside from trying and I think that sort of writing pretty clearly spelled out that I would not be off pills for long.

I write that I am on a diet which is supposed to make you feel healthy and whole. It is day three of this diet but I provide no specifications. I write that I am on the bus to New York from New Jersey and I am looking out at White Marsh where they force fish through channels, (a thing I imagined to be like pushing egg whites through a sieve) across industrial drums, and into a shallow and oily parkway. I write that this is on my right side. I write that I have this feeling that I've squandered everything and therefore to be hungry is my punishment. I write that vitamin B is my punishment so, obviously, I was on some post-pill health kick, which did not last long. This part is not written down, but later that night a man picked me up at the train station in Baltimore and I remembered meeting him coming out of the movies some years previously. He had commented on the film, saying it was so Bergmanesque, and then he took me to a party, that was intended to raise money for the Sandinistas in Nicaragua. Realizing that I knew this man, the one picking me up in Baltimore, from this earlier Bergman/Sandinista event instantly erased any possibility of staying off pills for very long.

I felt, in the car, like he had taken me down a peg or two because, after all, he was providing me a ride. My somewhat belittling rejection of him, which had occurred at the Bergman/Sandanista event, was coming back to bite me in the ass. I was not so high and mighty. I was not so healthy and whole. I tried to use his name a lot in our conversation while driving from the train station. It was a misguided attempt to regain the upper hand. He was fairly quiet and only spoke about his Ph.D. dissertation which, it seemed, was written in a foreign language. When the car stopped I thanked him. I said, "Thanks so much, Rob." He smiled and said, "I remember you really liked to party," as he opened a small velvet bag like you might use to carry jewels. Then he said, "My name isn't Rob," and he examined me from above his sunglasses. This is not in the notebook. In the notebook, after the bit about vitamin B, I wrote, *Go somewhere. Sit. Write a poem.*

JANUARY 1998: *Living inside this fiction, examine poem. I move around and make multiple fictions as houses. What is the dimension of such space? Echo reveals size. It can be very small, less a house or place to live but more "shrine." In one case a shrine is constructed from my limited knowledge of a foreign language. I translate this as "etc." It is constructed of wood, shiny paper, and red satin ribbon resting against a split-rail fence on Old Pecos Highway. It is the site of some unspeakable disaster. It is inevitable that I leave such monuments, even if they exist only in the notebooks. I make space. Or the things I wear retain the print of my body. Like the notebooks. Incorrect in facts (botching dates, names, etc.) but still the print of me. Recording. Like how I was in the house after my mother died and her nightgown was in the hamper below the sink. It held the shape of her figure. Her figure as if running and frozen like that.*

Sit. Write a poem. Those are the instructions, but miss the hard part. Meaning recovery, reconnaissance. If I erase everything else from my schedule, can I plan and locate tasks? I eliminate many things from my diet. I do this repeatedly.

Dairy, pills, wheat, alcohol, coffee, mustard, anything solid or cooked. I am on an elimination diet. It rotates and erases. In this erased knowing there is a universal language which for me resembles English. I write, *I must amend my diet. It is inflammatory and salty. Tomorrow will be better. Especially in terms of pills and ice cream.*

FEBRUARY 1998: *Driving to Durango with Sandra. Actually she drives and we listen to Glenn Gould in the rental car. We listen to this driving through the desert. I am experiencing a "hoarding mentality" and I have eaten waffles. Please write a poem. Please fly a poem. We continue on to Arizona in the rental car. We stop at a resort on a manmade lake of rock-milk in the desert. It looks like the moon. We are the only two people in the entire resort because it is off season. The hotel has over 500 rooms and we are alone there except for the staff who wait for us to arrive before cooking breakfast. They seem to know where we are at all times. We use the ice machines repeatedly because they seem so lonely.*

We drive to Tucson and pass the V. D. Gift Shop. In the Sonoran Desert, I go through a series of exhibits on local wildlife. They show us a twenty-five-year-old tarantula and the guide says, he is not long for this world. The names of insects repeat in my mind: Cloudless Sulfur Moth and Mariola Sonoran Nightshade. Now I am unsure if those are both insects or if they are some other type of wildlife. It is late when we drive through the white-baked acadia into Bisbee. An old man is selling prewar teaspoons out of the back of his car. Bisbee contains a multitude of hot tubs.

8

North again, guided spinning teaspoon compass of the rental car and eat dinner in

a pancake house where Sandra orders poached eggs and the waitress asks her if she

wants the eggs with the meat in 'em. Everywhere you look there are mined-out halves

of mountains. Some of them have plastic tarp squares over the open-sore parts and the

plastic is held in place by rocks. The wind ripples the plastic and there is dirt and dust—a

film of it—on everything including the food. I wear sunglasses all day and night because

the sandy earth blows into my eyes. I often forget I am wearing the sunglasses and at night

I find myself wondering why it is so dark. We stop at a bar in Globe, Arizona. Two men

sit down at our table. The four of us are the only people in the bar, not counting Jan, the

bartender. We order two beers. The two men say those are fancy-pants beers. They order

two Budweisers and pay the whole tab. They say their names are Jay and Jim. We order

several more rounds of beer. Pretty soon we don't care about making the effort to order

our fancy-pants beers and Jan just brings us four Budweisers. I want to leave but feel

heavy and sullen. I realize I am still wearing my sunglasses. Jay and Jim find all this

mysterious and sexy. I am bloated-sick from the pancake dinner and beer. Clearly none of

this is part of any sensible elimination diet.

Jay or Jim wants to put his arm around me. I say that I will allow this if he stops

breathing on me. We seem to have reached an understanding, but I am quickly unsure

of this arrangement because I am wearing less clothing than I would ideally like to be

9

wearing when sitting next to a sweating alcoholic. I am not sure how to get away from

Jay or Jim and his huge face swinging over me like a crane. I say I have to go to the

bathroom. I am in there for a while and then Sandra has come into the bathroom too

and we decide to immediately leave the bar and walk back to our motel. I am beginning

to equate true love with ordering pizza all the time. What's wrong with me? Can

anything help this? Getting fucked-up doesn't help. I know because I have had too many

irrational conversations with myself in public toilets. I have limitations in terms of what

I am able to write about the last week. This makes me question the sequence of events,

particularly details about how far and for how much time.

There are some things I only risk knowing inside poems. I mean in the poem, who cares how far we are from the motel?

The first time I wrote poems I was living on Cape Cod. What I mean is, the first time I worried about not writing poems I was living on Cape Cod. I typed six poems on an electric typewriter at the kitchen table. I didn't have any prescriptions, just beer. Sometimes I went out for drinks with my friends who were big drinkers. We were drunks together, which I was convinced was because most of us were getting over something. I lived with people who rotated in and out and worked for topless women landscapers. I slept in a loft that was so hot by 7 A.M. that I would have to get up. I ate lots of black bean burritos and the kitchen sink was so small you couldn't actually fit a dinner plate in there to clean it. I ate out of foil trays. I was very social in order to obtain alcohol. (Though I continued to drink alcohol, I began a strict no-sugar regime.) My notebook is full of initials. It is hard to remember who all those people were. I wrote, *The world is not well; C. is worse; D.*

owes money and his brother is mid-divorce; L. is sleeping on the street; A. is nearly broke; R. is an alcoholic; S. is stressed out about canned vs. cured olives; and of course T. can't get out of Greece but might in September with D.'s two thou which was my two thou but will pay his tuition instead of a flight to Argentina; P. joined the Army; and S. (the other one) is in love with a Mormon in Indiana. So I guess, in comparison, my two-week tension headache (which I had assumed was either a tumor or an aneurysm) is really nothing. In this list of initials I had also written, J. is a riot. But I now read that as J. is an idiot. That feels more true.

I rode my bike to the ocean and sat on the beach all day. I stayed up late at night watching *Mary Tyler Moore* reruns and went to Chicago on a trip.

JULY 1992: *This is the whole world.*

Lake Michigan was an ocean with a moon, pink/red/cookie. I stayed at a hotel, in a room called the Turkish Nook. On the airplane back to Boston, I made a list of things I needed to do: *clean up house, finish poem, read three books, go to Portland, OR.* I waited outside the public library on Boylston Street in order to meet Cathy. She came back out to the Cape with me and we went for a sailboat ride. When she left, I felt like I was eating ice cream really fast. Cold on the inside. In the notebook, I write that I watch her leaving, getting smaller in the distance. I write that but do not write that I feel sad. Instead I write *cold.* Then I write, *The writing has not been coming easy but I MUST STOP CRITICIZING MYSELF.*

JULY 1992: *This is the rolling world-ball.*

AUGUST 1999, NEW YORK: *Something about being here makes me want safe so bad. And sedatives. How can I write my life? The one I show to you? Can I see a movie? I saw Lora and Brenda and Eleni and Laird. Brenda makes the best pies. Laird*

said he was at the United Nations when Linda Gray from Dallas was made a special

ambassador to something. Everything is like a poem because a poem is secret and I am

the pleading medium. I stand here to make a translation, pleasing to everyone. I am

the special ambassador. The thing is to stop running everywhere (we are only at Sixth

Avenue). Distance, time, grape-colored silk charmeuse. How do you begin to know if you

are well-dressed? Where am I going? The chic cheese shops have swapped names. I didn't

even know it was Pretzel Time. I have walked across town on 23rd Street probably a

thousand times. So calmly past the Cerebral Palsy Society. Are you looking at my worlds?

I move into new houses and apartments all the time. I pack and unpack in a
frenzy. Everything has to be washed before it is packed. I take armloads of clothing
to the dry cleaner. I empty jars and wash them. I wash glasses and wipe down
everything including my pencils and spice jars. I wash my soap. When I unpack I
wash it all again. It is just a precaution.

JULY 1999: *I want my current, best world to be a good one. I make preparations for*
you. Everyday I do that.

JULY 1999, NOVA SCOTIA: *To a world you had known. Sandra and I went*
camping and slept in a new place each night. We were up on Dunvegan Bluff and the
night was windy. I walked far into the ocean. Gentle slope and ribbon-soft sand. Then
I wrote neatly with my finger. I decided I would try to write one true statement about

myself. Something which could be seen from a rescue plane. I could not think of anything for a long time. Then I wrote "I have no money" and while this is a true statement I didn't actually end up writing it at all. I gave up. I went to a dance instead in my long, orange hippie skirt with a man named Lawrence and his toupee. Then the camping trip was over and we went home to Sandra's house. We cleaned and cleaned—everything, the house, the sleeping bags, me outside in her yard in my bra bleaching the cooler.

Then I moved. Out alone and lived in a cabin on a salt marsh outside La Have. The very first day I biked eight miles to a bakery and bought an expensive jar of vanilla sugar. I was almost out of money but buying expensive sugar. I came home to the cabin. I had no running water or phone. I knew no one. I had no world. I only wrote phrases or single words in a notebook: *the ladder, blue rock, meat cove,* and then *motherhood, fortune, providence, the stars. depression, waves of corruption & rot. here is the false Italy.* Then I stopped and wrote, *July 20th, what is the big thing next to the sink in the basement?*

FIRST ENKOMION SEQUENCE

I.

me in front

      (round)

attempting to be more oval
(just start *thinking* like an oval)
the light pattern
altered
in an appearance of spontaneity
I was always on a diet

(SEE FIG. I)

somehow you are smaller and behind

me (as in crying, sitting on the floor)

my size adjusted

so you can at least

be visible are you visible yet

(I keep checking)

(FIG. 2)

behind again so as to push & not

roll away

is one a tiny bit smaller (though

standing) vein in forehead protruding

(not necessarily crying) move to

front move back

to front

back

to front

do not roll

(FIG. 3)

altered

& you become less

visible as predicted

but still kind of not the best

way to say, "where

did you go?"

imagine behind all three something

booming—big

bigger in spite of the hard-

working guilds (Renaissance perspective was not built in a day)

imagine it because

I will not draw it

(my size a protest)

(FIG. 4 IMAGINED)

over & away large but

rolling

distant

way beyond

the lawn, the basketball hoop & Dairy Queen

god

(FIG. 5)

II.

I try to see you

are you visible through something booming?

booming—big bigger in why were we never *ing*

as in crying, sitting, or becoming less visible as

if, well, imagine behind all this moving

a program that did not yet exist but in whose existence

I had taken an active interest

like photos accompanied by captions which report that

the photos are of real people engaged

in some activity

like the activity of being related

or eating sandwiches

you the she but

I (behind)

reports the first longing

accompanied by caption which identifies the subject as

"afraid of flying"

later this fear

is seen in analysis as more

the sense of rolling, rolling taking the place of flying

the therapist asking,

"has anyone considered the possibility that it was a suicide?"

III.

rolling

five thought bubbles intentionally
blank and opaque white
so that no one reads them
"soap bubble" or "apple"
after all they are round

I had taken on bubbles intentionally blank and opaque
the photos are for half of
us, I mean there is my half of the photo and
the half belonging to you
opaque white so that in some activity like
longing you appear real and round but
in about half you are more a
sash of light or some effect which disrupts
the taking of the photograph
you visible over my rolling around
booming
and then fading distant
the least visible, visible one

perhaps I swallowed too many capsules

me high up in the calm of kiddie cupcakes

like I will be okay now

but still rolling

losing control and catastrophizing

"that is it," the therapist says,

"your fear of human companionship,

your fear of flying,

of credit cards,

of puppets,

and clowns."

I write this down, *need human companionship and clowns,*

as an instruction

I had forgotten to mention weathermen

I also fear weathermen

"the absence of need is okay," the therapist says

"you are okay."

IV.

you put me in a pink gingham pinafore
my shell in a pink pinafore shell
it did size
because it wasn't a grow into
but basically grown out of
somehow more you than the me
visible
now I remember me putting you in the pink pinafore
as if you wore it and the matching
horrible underpants
out front, you smiling and in the horrible underpants
as if they were the greatest reason to be alive
I can't see anything around you
you grow and ask questions about sex and the SAT
my rolling visible to you but no one else and it is
me having sex
and the SAT
you ask, "how'd it go?"
like you did these things not me
me altered enough to be you
my absence is there in the cool pronouncement
"it was okay."

a picture of us was taken
and our mouths can't move in the photograph

but it is as if I am saying
okay
and you are saying
don't go

V.

it is as if you are saying

don't go because of the way my arm

is held by you

in the picture

distant but drawn

in

necessary to standing

that's it

it is as if we are holding each other

your half and my half balanced

to stand

back altered

the hinge or not

like where one

or both feel distant to visible

draws me in

always draws me in to ask

how far away were you?

where

were you going?

VI.

this was made by the shadow of

made by the sun on a wall

made with my memory as the only guide

it remains partly descriptive and partly

prescriptive

if you see this shadow

walk away

my life is something which can be learned

the instructions are:

seal my life

in this shell

the absence the outline of a shadow

which the sun has thrown on a wall

we eclipse perfectly

one

vita activa

and I am surprised and proud

because I have been drawing from memory

alone

you ask but I

VII.

that posture throwing out your chest
in a Halston gown with giant raglan sleeves,
giant browness of it something which was called draping
an invisible stitch along the bustline
the way the sleeves gathered at the wrist like
pajamas but with *draping draping* was described as never
pajamas I wondered about that word and later confused
it with *crepe* as in *crepe de chine*
a foreign language
you tapped the meaning into the palm of my hand
d-r-a-p-i-n-g and moved your mouth like Anne Sullivan
I could feel it in my whole body

foreign

language so the letters sound out and my

letters spell to say, *you are lying*

and I suddenly knew that I have actually seen

you do this *lying* but it was not *only* a bad thing

because you loved new draping

and would sneak out to smoke cigarettes but say

that you were doing laundry so smoking

cigarettes is what *doing laundry* meant

(or failed to mean) the way we got one thing for another

an economy about *draping* like money

and giant brown sleeves, a way of

standing with the heel of the right foot pushed

into the arch of the left "that posture throws out your chest"

which was the current funniest thing you said

and I told that as a joke to my best friend, "throws out your chest"

who was immediately hysterical

I made the letters in the palm of

her hand which was hard because

I could not remember how and she laughed even harder

hardly breathing it was the funniest

thing we had ever heard and the hand part tickled

it wasn't only a bad thing except

maybe

especially the part about laundry equaling

brownish or cigarettes which we then made

from typing paper and scotch tape

trying to make them the right size but for

our smaller hands and we put flour in the end

of these taped paper rolls and it was when we

decided to wear huge blouses and smoke

cigarettes and never do laundry

it was not, exactly, a thing to laugh about

and we were trying not to laugh because

when we laughed and were smoking the paper-roll

cigarettes, the flour went up our noses

your mouth was more down-like if you were lying
like about the laundry or cigarettes or about
money which you would get from him and make a smile
but turned down–type and I thought you were
signaling me like it isn't only bad
and no one else needs to know, least of all anyone in this car
anyway it was funny, the smile, and you wanted
some elegant gown I can't say it wasn't only
I thought you wanted things milkshake-bad
I thought it but didn't say it because I was sitting
on the sandy rug of a changing room floor
not playing with anything just trying

to suppress certain criteria for what was "enough"
(you had given up making the letters in my hand
"that's for babies," you said)
instead you went through a series of
slim skirts, brown, brownish, gray, grayish, modeling
we didn't have *enough* for all of them
or they were not long enough
or other types of *enough* (as in having a
winter coat, hair cut, the abandoned hair thingy)
you would say to him, "so then I will stop getting
my hair cut, if it is too much, but I
can't go to anyone else because so-and-so

is the only one who knows my hair" down-style
smile the whole time but you never stopped going to
so-and-so but sometimes my father would scream about
where does the money go and you would have the down-smile
slowly I learned about mythology and the tall tales
and how you could be punished and spend half the
year in the underworld which seemed very bad like
underwear something always getting dirty
needed laundering
so I asked my father what underworld was and he
said he was Jewish and there was no underworld
for him and I asked if there was underworld for you

.

and me and he said, "bullshit" so I didn't worry

quite as much about the cigarettes and laundry

and Halston and haircuts plus

losing all those hair thingys I responded

with something like naturalistic awkwardness

as in, my legs are as long (looking

in the dressing room mirror) or when I said

"I don't really want a milkshake," wanting it bad

habitually agreeing that no, my mother does not smoke, no way

he could interrogate but look nothing in my hands

nothing on my face except face, chest thrown out,

feet meeting strangely heel into arch, "no, I have nothing to hide" people were always questioning me

"where is your mother going?" and I sensed we had made some

sort of pact so I said nothing

I remembered you watching *Guiding Light*

you would say, I like that Mike, he is so solid.

so I liked Mike

I learned how to cook fancy dinner

I wore shoes

and had sex, took the SAT I read *Madame Bovary*

and began to remember you as listless, perfected in that way of laying on the couch

and I wondered where were you going?

VIII.

believe me
high up safety
the dread of
such semihuman types
(clowns, weathermen)

I am on the lookout

things growing the high top of her strawberries
dress the neighbor boy has to have *some* pants on it *is* a birthday
after all, tiny strawberries mixed and checks that close the heart
sit on the steps (pounding) I stood shining in sun-
shine, he was too young for long pants, these snap easier
a blur in the top to bottom misses the hummingbird

stuck there, pressed against stucco and prints, hummingbird
in the sunshine red and green with small strawberries
growing on the front of her dress up and near, easier
to recognize I was told to do certain things on my birthday
(do not touch the bow) blinking, inside what was growing to the sun
I was told *and then lean into the stucco*, a cake rounded twice as a heart

extra cream, please, which I have memorized, like the camera, by heart
falling from the highest part of her dress, drop to feed sweets to the hummingbird
this does not appear in the photo wish toward the edge's sun
with no spilling and who holds the camera? the perfect house, strawberries
survived air raids and the occasional birthday
meanwhile in the cool kitchen the cream and cake is arranged easier

it places us a little distance from the stucco steps, easier
to make out, the middle is me and my grandmother, circles of a heart
except she is younger, mouth like a small violet, can't be my birthday
but my mother's birthday, the air raids real and quick-heart hummingbird

the boy who is too young moves out of the photo, reaching strawberries
which my grandfather tore out in the 1960s, there was just not enough sun

it can't be me in the photo, meaning that day why was there so much sun?
I don't know either except to know that the photo makes it easier
or rather the sun makes the photo easier and I can say look at the strawberries
and know that I cannot be in the picture, it is her heart-
shaped cake waiting on the stucco just past the invisible hummingbird
you don't have them anymore, sun headaches or birthday

parties the little boy who is too young was there on the steps on her birthday
wearing snap-front pants and flattened in snap-shot sun
the old-fashioned flash circling his head a hummingbird
her face which says *I can't touch the bow or it is easier*
not to complain about this small checked dress tied like a candy heart
easier to think that there will be cake and not air raids, waiting away
    from the strawberries

secretly eating strawberries on her birthday
into all her heart a bow tied to be tight in the sun
no one made it any easier and she remains, for me, a flicker, the hummingbird

I think at nine she might have said, "I won't wear this outfit"
but standing next to her father, what might be her ninth birthday or the garage, you
see the coat carelessly thrown, she is looking away and down, stoic and away
traveling on some airy plains not Flushing, Queens, just got a new Betty and Dick
        book (please stay)
(please read), far away animals to color, the winking panda, "just wishing everything
that's fine . . . /for someone who's reached the age of nine, with love, Mother"

meaning these two are together with some regularity love and Mother,
my mother lined them up, the Walt Disney Paint Outfit
or Make Your Own Charm Jewelry because at nine she did everything
alone, gravity of being alone, a timid jury of dress-ups, the dolls, you
remember the Betty and Dick books? a notorious case where Betty and Dick get to stay
in Chicago—"best hotel in the world, the Stevens!"—the next day Dick and Daddy
        went away

while Betty and her Mother visited the Cradle—home away
from home for orphaned babies—and Betty fell so in love with them she asked
        Mother
if she could bring them home to play with her and her dolls, to stay
"you can imagine," my mother says to herself, "Betty's mother was a serious fact
        evaluator outfit
and told Betty, 'We must move on to Tulsa.'" Tulsa—a real Western City! you
meet Indians who speak English and have gay, colorful costumes with blankets
        and everything!

Betty thought the Indians had funny names, Johnny Rain-in-the-Face and everything
reminds me (because Betty and Dick seem happy) that my little mother couldn't
    want to get away
every bit of her too-small coat used up, every inching bit and then, unexpectedly, you
see, Betty became unpredictable at the oil wells which were meant to be educational,
    my mother
was nine and insisted on a trial in judging Betty's bad behavior, the jury characterized
    in outfit
of matching blink-eyes and tweezed-over yarn-curls, but why, at nine, does my
    mother stay

arguing? on what basis is Betty becoming unpredictable? refusing to stay
in Tulsa? wanting to go to Hollywood? Betty would like to say, "fight how everything
is diminished," though what she really says is something about the "Hollywood
    Indian's outfit"
only she doesn't say it because my mother does the talking, playing Betty and
    examining away
at the witness, poor, unpredictable, irrational Betty, the Betty whom my mother
hates because she gets to go to Hollywood, see large cameras, lights called klieg
    lights you

may wonder what the jury made of such conflicting documents, you
ask how a nine-year-old girl can hate Betty, after all, she's only Dick's sister, getting
    to stay
in hotels but cross examination into the birthday card accompanying the book *with*
    love, Mother
proved an impossible criteria for choosing witnesses, my mother is nine plus, up
    until now everything

has done the opposite of *with love, Mother* rather something absent or away
is what her mother really wrote, when she wrote it herself and not Daddy writing
   for the whole outfit

my mother's coat was too small, so ugly she hated it not the right outfit you can
   see that
right away, Betty and Dick leave Hollywood for Miami where they see an orange
grove and everything while my little mother cut an *L* shape from the coat's back
   but had to wear it anyway

above the dressing table a cereal box–sized Jesus
she sits to put on one shoe then the other, the bed warm as an anchor
she is wearing an electric blue blouse saving
the blouse for special occasions saving
the jacket too and everything that is saved for a future spring
coat (you never know what shoes will go with that) "I am going to scream"

and "I beg your pardon" she might say but it is not her who goes to scream
only wanted the "now" concluded wanted and prayed "Jesus
let me out let me," attaching the rhinestone lucky clover clip-ons, "let this spring
be the one let my life get smaller, small as a love hotel, an alley, an anchor"
she reported "I wanted to have now concluded and stop saving
myself and patterns and cloth in the corners of pillowcases," saving

old handbags, the old round dial radio, or the double event saving
the more or less you know about me or her she began to scream
not on the outside but in not fitting the one shoe just right and how long can she
    be saving
an electric blue, Peter Pan–collared blouse, the savior Jesus
I mean Jesus she had been saving for so long and careful of the corners anchor
them down with the smallest bit of spare cloth, the whole house a loaded spring

of saving a resolve to hold out until after her mother was well the following spring
would be a good time for her to leave home, etc., her father said saving
the receipt for the week's milk delivery, her father—he was an anchor—

always did the cooking and shopping, too, because her mother's recovery (she
    did scream)
never happened, the old woman would say, "my nerves" Jesus
was not to blame said her father, Jesus was busy saving

helpless children in India and only helped those who were saving
themselves, he told my mother, "by next spring
Mother should be right as rain, praise Jesus!"
my mother thought she could perhaps go on saving
the blue blouse because for twenty-nine years her mother had "the nerves" and
    to scream
did nothing just one shoe then the other in her good blouse she felt that house anchor

and dressed to meet a person who could look at the rhinestone, lucky clovers,
    loosen the anchor
she conjured a place with rows and rows of fine electric blue blouses without saving
bits of material for patching (she never could sew) she made him the one who
    would scream
out her name, understand the lucky-clover ear-drops and spring
full-formed, ready for her style, not invisible to others but she went on saving
certain things boy, did she buy it, straight off the back of the cereal box, Jesus!

Jesus was the anchor for she remained there *and* a virgin
saving herself and all that went with it saving the package deal in the
spring she moved to an apartment they painted French-like in white & gold, it was
    a scream

completely out of the question, the quilted bag, ferry boat, the baby
all of it out now more because of the heavy bags and ferry boats, the yellow
little baby she was looking for protection in the form of something to do, smoking
remained a bright option, only now and then she thought, but it was almost every
    day in the park
wandering the new production around, perfectly in white
towel-like softness, growth rate inching up, decidedly still soft, but also a stranger

she turned around, she was always turning, posed for the photo, on the ferry with
    a stranger
prolonged lapse, the moment fell away all around the baby
the stranger who was a baby, curled pea shoot wrapped in white
like some kind of bandages, she feels it is strange to have bandaged up a baby
    the yellow
sun it is against the sun that the baby is packaged just like the days the walk the park
the day a day for a day and the baby is some sort of prize for waking, patching up,
    smoking

was she accompanied by the one who takes the photograph? from here it is just
    her smoking
we would be talking about sharply cropping the photo, removing the car with its
    balding stranger
or making the photo of three places, one on the ferry, the others in the hospital and
    the park
the one where she began screaming and they agreed that no one could bear that
    and a baby

is coming so she proudly went to sleep sweetly bandaged in the yellow
daisy nightie specially selected and the whole room posed as knowledgeable and white

the photo in the park, after thirty minutes or so, shows her sickly white
poaching on a bench, officially shivering in August under her camel hair coat,
    smoking
of course later she laughed, light-hearted, "did I have a dress with yellow
flowers? I have no idea who this is," she looked at this part of the picture, "a
    stranger?"
she said like it was a detective trip, "I wish I knew who was holding the baby
in this one. I can't imagine that I didn't have my eye on her," but she is alone,
    shivering in the park

it is all excusable, her kidneys, the smoking, the stranger in the park
no one said a word about it later, she always wore sunglasses with egg shapes, white
and dark how do we make the ID definitive? "must have mixed it up," she said,
    "the baby,
I never left my baby even for a moment's discretionary income, smoking.
I was not a stranger," she said but she got stranger and stranger
claimed to posses a criminal record but not for leaving a bandaged-up yellow

baby, she said, or something to that effect like she was a perfect mother, standing
    in that yellow
daisy-print nightie, packing up sandwiches, taking the children for walks in the park
repeating things like "eat that liver" and "don't talk to the stranger"
pronouncing the best stage actor and her only mission to white-
wash, wash-up, wake and watch, it was never her still smoking
in spite of the warnings and nearly all the bystanders forgot about the coat in
    August, the baby

what if you were the baby? the one barely visible beside a yellow
daisy nightie, saw her smoking secretly behind the laundry soap or in the park
what if in a perfectly produced white-sun photograph, you are the stranger?

what if you are the baby? the stranger? the center of photographs and answer
to the question, "how could any of this have happened?" or the crisis moment
of a proletarian novel? what if you were the one who had traveled?
the girl who bought five copies all in the first week? what if you were first?
the one she was obliged to do it for? bound to have the conversation with? to set
  out in a snow
storm? and the one practically ignored? the one who mixed up the dressing (little

salad maker)? or the child asking, "do you think this is a good life, any of you?"
  (the little
bit we all could agree on) the one exaggerating casualty reports or a particularly
  tactless answer
to the unnaturally green veneer he chose for a coffee table? what if you were
  the one out in snow
watching cars coming out of what if you could not reproduce? (the illustrations,
  moment-
by-moment whispering instructions) the one solving the problem of sudden loud
  noise first?
(before the others even hear, "hey, listen to this")? or the one who traveled

to the Medici palace in December? (the three liter bottles are near empty and I
  traveled
all this way to find that what was not agreed upon was the most important part, little
use) what if in the pictures, and outside of them, they all look untrustworthy? first
just spacey, but then more ceramic, uncertain, completely dazed, unable to answer

even the easy ones about corkscrews and film stars (not the sort of thing that in
    the moment
inspires a hell of a lot of confidence) or one more time when a motorcycle appears
    in the snow

we don't take the ride, at least that is how I remember it kept walking in the snow
in a purple hat, wherever the hell we were going, and what if all of it had traveled
into the basement? and you are the one to find hundreds of little pictures, separate
    moments
people you don't know but she is crying over hundreds of little
people and you say "do you know these people?" and she means "no" but is crying
    "no answer"
what if you just want the Tot-Finder Fire Sticker put up? or something because you
    are the first

one at school and learning about something, fire safety, and you ask her, "first
can you do this for me, put this up for me?" because you are too small and the snow
has collected on the window panes, it should go in the window, you say but there
    is no answer
and what if you were then convinced living without this red sticker would mean
    they traveled
for nothing and you were all going to die in a fire and this kept you up at night a little
worried about fire, natural disasters, bombs, and brain cancer all which can happen
    any moment

unquestionably due to conditions or to something food- and soil-based because
    "at any moment,"
she says, "everything could fall apart," or it has already and she is crying over
    the photographs first

saying nothing and what if you said "don't cry; it will be alright" even though
    you're the little
one and would like the fucking Tot-Finder Fire Sticker in the fucking window
    because the snow
is pretty high against the windows? and you are sure that if there was (they traveled
often) a fire or natural disaster or brain cancer well then no one would ever know
    you or answer

and you would call and there would be no answer, wait a moment
perhaps they had traveled and forgotten to tell you first
and you set out in light snow walking to get away, yeah, you have some issues, a little

if she had said, "this is restricting" or "I would prefer the title
of being restricted" but it always lurked, another view trade
for the fact that this seemed like the perfect home, collapse
on the perfect sofa (it was before all the smaller furniture), stability,
a way of her knowing that the sofa was always the sofa change
out of those swimsuits before you sit anywhere soft petal

green sofa she sits waiting for the work assigned with all the speculation of a petal
we come in quietly and the sofa does not seem to equal home but the title
mother she sits there or is lying under a blanket small change
since the morning "arms length" is how she says it, preferring to trade
our wet suits for her not listening to a story about the pool, not stability
for a mortgage or some equation we can not imagine yet so collapse

this is not such an easy part the collapse
the way we have walked in mud and clover petal
careful not to dirty the couch (it is part of the trade-off) stability
of our nation depends on hers, the one known by the title
mother, the one that is remote, I am cut off from this authority, this trade-
off is not in the best interest of our country, in the country of cleaning up
    and to change

for supper out of those suits, the only marker now that we wish not to change
the way we know we are from a different country, our country of collapse
because the way she wants one thing for another is trade
but now being perfectly quiet is in the contract, she thinks we wear the petal

bits on purpose that this means we will not be quiet or respect her title
but it is really hard to get the clover bits off wet feet and maintain stability

so on each foot and knocking the water from our ears, the straight chair for stability
we came in to say that we want to live in another country change
countries (she is still on the sofa under a blanket) we like how you know in the title
that the people live in another country like Madeline books and we collapse
near her feet we like that Madeline lives in France a petal
sticks to the sofa or the adventures of Master so-and-so which we read aloud and
    want to trade

he lived in Italy we said and we would like to trade
live there too, with Master so-and-so and the clever dog but she says, "there is no
    stability
in Italy" she is pale and absentmindedly removes the petal
"if you go Italy and want to be little girls there with a clever dog it is not so easy
    to change
back. you might not have the perfect home. your perfect home might be ruined
    and collapse.
you girls don't know that you can't change the stories only the title"

which she says doesn't matter but we know all the titles and how to trade
one thing collapses and you get another sort of stability
we know we must change to Italy, the other one, and she simply holds up a silvery
    clover petal

um, the pictures, the ones in which she is wearing make-up and stilettos
something bigger than the city or choosing fresh-cut lamb chops—a root canal
the kind performed over and over, a building from the inside, a real-life
morality play, no one gets out free, not the smokers or the wintergreen
gum chewers, not much forgiven, raincoats all deeply resembling the newest
color and winter shapes, shaped like a few winters' ago, only gray

if I saw cosmetics or the small cosmetics bag she often had, but too small, it was gray
shoes, gray and silver waffle-iron steps, the moving faster her in stilettos
it isn't easy to say how far we had walked, she was silent, mourning the newest
way of losing it, it was booming all around and he had been booming, it is only
      root canal—
not the Holocaust which of course nothing really was, chewing Wrigley's wintergreen
gum I was aware that nothing in my life would be the Holocaust but what was
      that? in real life?

the Holocaust? we wouldn't have been able to tell you, riding that train was real life
her hand (right) offering the green papered bit, emerging from a bullet of leather-gray
glove was not as soft anymore or she could have said, with wintergreen
gum disappearing and reappearing, "my hands are not so soft" tapping stilettos
against the grim gray slide train, don't let this happen to you, this awful root canal
which was said not to be the Holocaust but reaching into her life, pulling and newest

pulling out of the station and pulling off her heavy coat, I am pulling off my newest
best coat, a coat I hate and have tried to lose on buses and skating trips taking it out
      of real life

to make it someone else's life, I left it at Mrs. Gage's house, but it was a singular,
  ugly root canal
of an overcoat but like Sunday, root canal, fists and yelling—no Holocaust, just
  stilettos
she read a magazine folding the square of silver paper, flaking away the shine until
  it was gray
she was the prettiest (almost ever) in her gray sweater and clicking a slice of
  wintergreen

gum, you can't say a word about this, (she is laughing) about this wintergreen
candy to your sister, she is too young and could choke easily choking becoming
  the newest
non-Holocaust event but still bad and I promise and she crosses her legs, the stilettos
point forward dangerous, a pain is through me, is thinking these shoes are more
  about real life
than anything, her hands feel soft, her sweater is soft but wiry and mossy gray
I look at her too long, she says, "I sense I have learned something on the way
  to the root canal"

if I was looking to learn something on the way to the root canal
I knew I had learned to chew gum and not swallow, put it back into the Wrigley's
  wintergreen
paper but we were not looking to learn something and the final station floor was
  sad and gray
it snowed and I had a hot cheese sandwich later, in Union Square, in my newest
best coat, with a ripe pickle spear and my mother only smoked after all it was real life
and ate a frosty dish of yellow vanilla ice cream she said, "I have to get out of these
  stilettos"

she removed the stilettos on the train home from the root canal

sitting with me just like real life and eating lifesavers—wintergreen

she fingered my newest and best coat, laughing, "this is terrible, even if it's gray"

and she shut the door behind her
she pretended to be worried
she immersed herself in household tasks
she left on the 8:38 train
she took the baby away from the nurse
she brought her in when there was company

concerned that it was not good enough for company
or no one wants to hold her
"you are just like the daughter of old (blank) the fisherman from (blank)," said
  the nurse
she was shattered and sobbing and everyone worried
she took it as a stupid insult resolved to make the train
the child became the sole object of her resentment, oh, and the household tasks

it wasn't so much the household tasks
she learned first to make spaghetti sauce for fancy company
on Thursdays she was driven to the morning train
satisfy cravings for (blank) or (blank) and instead of trying to put it out of her
mind she cherished it, to suffer, never missing an opportunity to be worried
it was the way the child curled round the nurse

which ultimately provided the peaceful lament not so much the nurse
herself or the way that the nurse had special ways of accomplishing tasks
for instance she boiled and ate squirrels caught in the park which worried

the father and was unsightly if ever there was company

but it was the child not crying for her, her

own mother or something about how she would say to the nurse, I must

 make this train

which was a recrimination not the train

but the child's face like a pinwheel circling the nurse

and she bit her lip and left for the wrapped parcels and new silver shoes her

favorites were stilettos, one day she saw a small nightgown with embroidery,

 accepted the task

to conjure up the child, be suddenly transported to the child's company

like any mother she saw she could buy this small nightgown but she worried

was it too small? the child's dimensions uncertain she worried

had she seen the child sleeping in a nightgown? she boarded the train

she knew she must not worry, a small nightgown would be sweet for when there

 was company

and how could she know if the child wore nightgowns? it was the damn nurse

who dressed her and added special scented flakes to the laundry, performing

 those tasks

she learned to make dinners like chicken with apricots, thinking of the nurse, I will

 get rid of her

the child loved her nurse and worried, as she left, *who will do all the washing and*

household tasks? but the mother stopped taking the train to Lord & Taylor, or to

 movies, no one

spoke of the nurse except years later to tell the story of cooking squirrels, as a joke,

 to company

he knew whose gentle hand was at the latch, who stared at him
plainer, plainer she had no intention to marry
or, more likely, *if I have no chance at one thing, let me have another*
legs that went to here she had a sidelong view of everything
refuting examination of the center but more interested in the baffling around it
    something
like tulle that was impossible to iron, *why I have been a butterfly!*

she tells herself the high-brow intention of a butterfly
but the landscape did not contain a way *out*, only *toward* him
toward what was possible in small spaces, something
like private or sequestered stations such as to marry
potentially middle class with the pursuant scale problems, everything
advertising some hand cream or another

corrupt access the desire to have it all another
idea which didn't occur to her she was engulfed, a twitching butterfly
of middle-class ambition without work to do everything
pointed toward the three choices: nurse, nun, teacher in choosing him
she was on a trip to the outer limits of such wormy circumstance, to marry
to say, *I fall, I flow, I melt,* which drew something

to her, mirroring the amorous image, brought something
to her, blushing and secret, exhibitionist in a spring coat which allowed another
look at those legs, they lost their practical power to walk in flattering heels but
    to marry,

that could be done like a moment of hypnosis, moment the butterfly
emerged as in *I am nowhere held together but in this is a lovely big house*, it was him
looking down or it was him journeying, her faithful, if you thought everything

she did appeared to be faithful, for a long, long time everything
was adorable, intoxicated upon flower beds, new shower curtains something
like lunch had tremendous meaning, all this in an anxiety of him
in making a vow so that something would happen, another
set of floral slipcovers, chock-a-block with yellow lilies and butterfly
so special we could hardly sit on them, the horror of spoiling it, the impulse to marry

which was something she had apparently never entertained, questions of who she
    would marry
were settled easily (threw an engagement present into the storm drain once)
    "everything
was so clear," she said, which meant that she had chosen not to marry x or y,
    light butterfly
of thought, never even considered it really but made a vow so that *something*
might happen, perhaps, a kind of tapestry or freedom to buy expensive Italian
    shoes, another
choice perhaps, something continuously underpredicted like the way we saw him

tell her don't tell jokes if you don't know how, but remember that she had agreed
    to marry
she had chosen one thing (so many rooms) over another and everything
but something had not been projected: the life of docile reception, being beautiful
    languid butterfly

less vocal part of the body responds to error, days, years
he says, "wait a moment while this kicks in" touch to his gentle egg
yeah, it's getting there and the rest continue eating wishing to get out early
maybe or she holds out a plate of tomato, slices of white bread, brown
crust shiny as a casing, twisting off a bottle of Wild Turkey with the hem of her blouse
he says, "isn't anyone else drinking?" the rest laugh, detecting change, television

back at the motel it is decided, "the girls need to get out" overheard over television
he waits for it to kick in and then is skeptical, we have not been there in years.
waiting, "just call them and we can have a day," she says and waiting he climbs her
    impossible blouse
"get ready to visit a horse farm," she says in front of the television, rests on the cot
    like an egg
no one here has a choice about horse farms or leaving behind the motel television
    and brown
bed covers he is waiting by the car, smoking a distance from it, we are early

part of the job is stopping the responding to error early
enough but no one wants that job he wants the waiting job, television
is the job she really wants but the reading-a-magazine job will do, passing brown
bared tree branches sharing a few lifesavers, "we are driving for years,"
he says, smoking and circulating, barrel-chested, boomed out behind the egg
or the steering wheel, she drinks a Coke, looks down, has imagined a spill through
    her blouse

we are driving for years then stop not at horses but *hoffbrau*, I am sleeping
    in her blouse

"you missed it, kiddo," he says smoking again, circulating again, fell asleep early
she carries me pressed into the blouse, softly like I'm broken bits, egg-
shell, he says "*hoffbrau*" singing it and I wonder *is hoffbrau a horse on television?*
another man and woman are there with us and say, "we must have seen you two years
ago" and the food is something else here the walls paneled and beer brown

he says, "isn't anyone else drinking?" and he is waiting for the better part, the brown
bottles of beer appear and the end of a high skirt, small garters, wedding cream blouse
where something else is disappearing, arms, legs, years
greasy sausages are served and he is waiting, *yeah*, he thinks, *it will kick in anytime,*
    early
to bed and you get this waiting and sausages, the push-up blouse and television
there are potatoes and creamy pickles, the sticky glasses and hard-cooked egg

early to rise and it's a day full of waiting, smoking, circulating, wake-up bacon egg
breakfasts for the first two weeks that I worked at the *hoffbrauhaus*, it was a beige
    and brown
speckled horse in my mind, didn't remember being there as a kid, the
    motel, the television
until coffee was in the part of the body responding to error, days I ironed my pastry
    of a blouse
hundreds of miles from the familiar, waiting to finish up, marry the ketchups early
get out of the uniform waiting for it to kick in, waiting for what would spill out of
    being nineteen years

old ah! those marvelous years! timing rows of white pills, the perfect egg
early physical signs suggested waiting simply meant that trees were more often brown
than any happier and waiting I twisted the top off inside my greasy blouse
    comforted by television

and the sun, 6 A.M. or so, sleep away likeness and something which collects like salt
made you look, perhaps meaning we had to get up not to time the roast
but because the phone was ringing, it was her mother calling about a wasp's nest
something not unusual at 6 A.M., in spite of disaster and storm
"where are you, Mom?" she asks and my grandmother answers that she is in
    the kitchen
"she is frightened," my mother says, "she is frightened," she mouths a sour

face, so hot even at 6 A.M. it is likely we will evaporate everything cold is curdled sour
"what do I do with the wasp's nest?" "wait until we get there, Mom" the very salt
of the earth, my grandfather, thoughtlessly died without cleaning up the wasp's
    nest, the kitchen
he mapped a silent burden, often behind the wheel, left the Tropicana roses to roast
away in the yard while we dress and eat and drive hidden, pressed to the storm
my mother weeping hidden shoulders but thundering like a wasp's nest

my mother is silent for the first time, except for weeping, ominous and high-up as
    a wasp's nest
feel tighter than tight shoes, in a nutshell, we are in the too small car, stalled on the
    bridge, a sour
sky, the street mirrored dark in the sky a slow claiming of blue it will storm
she cries about this and about the slow bridge, she thinks that she is crying,
    sweating salt
swimming against the exhaust, sick with exhaust, sickly crying, "what if she forgot
    the roast!"

he says that he hopes it rains, that we need that and she sobs harder, wasps
    in the kitchen!

after the bridge, the slightest things wrong all the way (he said "what's wrong
    with the kitchen?")
"want to get ready for (we must have looked pretty stupid) Mass?" she says, eyes the
    wasp's nest
it is easier to understand only crying or quickly making gravy for the roast
but suddenly she is overly efficient and saying that the candy should be in dishes
    she is not sour
more like a threatening phone call, in the kitchen grandmother talks a blue streak,
    throwing salt
on the potato salad and eggs, "up all night. my nerves are shot. shot through. with
    this storm."

the priest in the living room has examined the wasp's nest—secretly, I hope for the
    storm
the heat almost beyond anything, Aunt Margaret says, "he was a dear man," comes
    in the kitchen
and pours a plastic cup half Canadian Club, half ginger ale and a glass of water
    doused with salt
"this is for your grandmother, God bless her, and saltwater for your dad, out with
    that wasp's nest"
but I can't imagine how to drink the warm water and salt, I stir the sour
smelling potato salad, the potatoes still warm and the whole room stifling, baking
    the roast

everyone else comes in after Mass and they don't eat any of the roast
the clouds brocaded into sky, unmoving, resisting the storm

my grandmother, after five cocktails, head of curlers, resting her elbow in the
    cooling beef, sour
and sharp tongued and Mother unable to eat or speak standing like a wedge
    in the kitchen
door, slim and with momentum like she will move from any human, closer
    to the wasp's nest
closer to saying she can't believe it, can't live like this, can't stand up, but instead
    retrieves the salt

the salt, that's what grandmother wants, elbow firmly in the roast
her head buzzing like a wasp's nest preparing for the coming storm
unable to see my mother in the kitchen, reaching for the bottle, for the glass,
    awfully sour

PART TWO

I write *what is the big thing next to the sink in the basement?* because it is a contest on the radio. It is the What-is-the-Big-Thing-Next-to-the-Sink-in-the-Basement? Contest and people call in with answers. Next they have a woman who tells you how long any given food has until it goes bad without refrigeration. Deviled eggs are the first things to go in a picnic she says. "Hmm, deviled eggs," says the announcer, "good to know."

I am interested in the radio. Call-in shows and helpful-tips shows. On the radio I find out about how to get shrimp peeler jobs and then about how two people killed a small child and then that a diabetic is meant to eat often but not too much.

This is a watery place. Roughly everywhere is a marsh or bay or channel or river or canal. I suppose people used to make homes on water for very practical reasons. I have no such reasons. This is a place dominated by harbors and basins and piers and bogs and wet trees and it seems like everything is wet and the laundry never gets dry all the way.

Today I saw a girl by the side of the road catching butterflies. I could see her arms swinging there on the road not catching butterflies but dangling a badminton racquet. I was wondering how she could play badminton on such a windy day: there were white caps and gulls hanging in the sky. The girl was swinging a badminton racquet and I walked up to her and she said, "I would like to go to Toronto. Are you going to Toronto?"

"No." I said. "I am writing a poem."

"Well it is where I am going," she said. She seemed very small, maybe fourteen years old. At a distance I had thought that she was nine or ten and maybe a boy. A car flashed by us and she ran and hid behind cattails. The car passed and she returned. I wanted her to speak again.

"I have never been to Toronto," I said.

"Do you have a car?" she asked.

"No," I said, "but I think I could get one."

"That's not really going to work," she said. "I was planning on leaving right now, so unless you can get a car today, I don't think it would work out." I felt sad even though I didn't want to leave for Toronto. She seemed clean and had shiny hair. She looked very seriously at me as if weighing my viability as a method of getting to Toronto. Then she said "sorry," kissed my mouth, and ran down toward the water. It was very windy, a constant wind. I felt sedated.

You look at and touch this rounded world.

I am not a scientific person. Science feels large and booming. The proving. Hurricanes, for example. Considering hurricanes is the kind of thing that puts me behind. I fear bad weather because there isn't much to the house I am living in. It is over water like a houseboat.

The radio says that doctors removed half of a girl's brain. It is true. They are concerned that she might not ever be able to speak.

On the radio is a story. A woman named Margaret had a large lawn ornament. It was a large cow lawn ornament. In spite of the fact that it was life-sized and hard to move around (according to Margaret), one day this cow lawn ornament was stolen. Turns out that when this happened Margaret went on the radio saying how she had a cow lawn ornament stolen and the woman who had sold Margaret the cow lawn ornament in the first place was listening. Her name was Irene. She had a large stock of life-sized, cement cow lawn ornaments. She called in and said that she would replace the life-sized, cement cow lawn ornament free of charge. Irene donated the thing but then there was the matter of getting the replacement lawn ornament, made of cement, to Margaret's lawn nearly 500 miles away. Unquestionably a fork lift was needed. Someone with a fork lift had to bring the lawn ornament the 500 miles to the house where Margaret, without her beloved lawn ornament, lived. And, lo and behold, if Cameron Fife, of Florenceville, didn't call in and say that he had a forklift and a truck and would bring the life-sized, cement cow lawn ornament to Margaret's place and, right then and there on the radio, the whole thing was set up. Margaret now takes good care of her new life-sized, cement cow lawn ornament and has called it Daisy. She says that she has done this because Daisy is a nice English name. Irene, on the line again, is quick to point out that she and her husband and mother-in-law (who does the painting, of the life-sized lawn ornaments) can make any kind of cow, and "If you have a prize-winning cow," Irene says, "Mother is very good at copying the markings."

I take out my notebook and write *you can never be too careful*. Maybe the whole lawn ornament thing will be a lesson to me about how you can't be too careful. This is something that I am afraid of so I can make myself think *hurricane* and remember to be careful. I will just remember the word. *Hurricane*. There is a nurse on the radio now saying that very many people are not properly medicated for pain. "People die in pain," she said. This is believable to me. She says that people think that they will be perceived as problematic if they request pain relief. "Or," she says, "people believe that the ability to suffer is important." This sickens the nurse and I agree.

This is a hurricane world.

In the movies or in novels, the person you identify with, if female, is always beautiful. Even if it is strangely beautiful or wickedly beautiful. She is not decidedly pear-shaped or having a brow which extends clear across her forehead, weak chinned, or hippy. This is just an observation. If I am going to write these poems about you and you are my heroine, then I have to think about these things. What did you look like? I have decided to have three characters. Two are female. One is a disaster.

I decide that in the poem you are right-handed. I chose the right hand. Right hand dominates ideas of holding or navigation. The hand moves but the movement comes from the forearm. It is a turning. It is a hard gesture to explain if you do not know it. It is a movement like producing a beautiful apple, a very large-sized apple, from a sack or perhaps from behind my back. It is a look-what-I-have look. Look-what-I-have-brought-to-you, you-are-lucky-I-am-here look. I watch you, getting happy to see a precious large thing produced. But, right now, it is not exactly that movement. It is more of an anchor. It holds like anchoring. How could you know this steady anchoring movement which comes up like an offering but stays just short of a giving and is only a holding? This may not seem admirable. It will perhaps indicate that I am aging. While I am located here, anchored here, in an accomplishment that is not clear to you. Because this is me walking. I am walking on a sand and stones path and the grass is growing damp and so I have pulled up this long skirt and I have done this in a small, anchoring twist. And you may be thinking that this movement, on the right side of my body, was a playing and something offered, but it turned into a holding and this has passed between us.

I use this aspect to say *you were the grown-up*. You are thinking. It is undeniable. You think *trees, a large bone of indistinguishable origin* (we are some meters away from the tree, the bone-like object). You are thinking. You think that time is of the essence, but you think it like this: *I have to get going*. I write you going. Rushing. Your purse flying open. Gum packages spilling out. You are agitated and applying a lipstick that I have tried on in your bathroom. It is called Ginger-Peachy. It sounds happy like we should have always been going to the beach.

Where are you going?

I would like to get on with it. We could possibly agree that I am anchored. You are correct, I have been aging the whole time. I have spent more time aging than you might imagine. You remember me one way, but here I am another. I am playful around people. You wouldn't have guessed that. I try to look forward a little. *That is not a bone at all* you begin to think. I know what you are thinking. I know because I made you right-handed.

"Tell me," I begin, "about what happened." You laugh. Then you deepen. I take this cue and say, "Don't dismiss the details, don't crawl away." You seem quite long and cool. "Tell me first about my eyes."

"I don't know," you say.

I turn to you, repeating the twisting forearm and anchor a bit further, and I do. I tell you. I say, "You should." "Yes," you say. "Usually." But then I say, "Quiet," and you are, and we approach the birds fishing on the water's grabbing edge. We stand and I hear you, hot and deepening. I do not know if you enjoy the silence. I am losing interest in birds. You say nothing. I wait and the birds are still fishing and then I drop anchor. I am there.

I whisper, "I need a bath." I leave the water's edge and move inside the cottage. Start a fire to heat water. As I drag the basin out onto the deck overhanging the water, the loons arch together and raise to gain flight and then they are flying.

The water begins to simmer and this is warm enough on such a hot day. "I need to have a bath," I say. You seem very serious. You are floating and also serious. The ocean is moving out from the place where the birds have just taken up flight. "Do you understand?" I ask you. You remain silent. "You need to leave now," I say, and you are unmoved though floating. "I always bathe alone," I say and now you move, not toward me or away.

"You have blue eyes," you say.

"I don't have blue eyes," I say, but then I look at you, slim and dark and floating and I am not sure. "I wish to get the bath before my water is cold," I say, and then I say, "I've made you selfish and right-handed."

You say, "I was right-handed."

I say, "Exactly."

I have become economical with the water, using no more than three gallons for a bath. This has gotten to be very routine, the three-gallon bath. Perhaps it sounds like three gallons is a lot of water, but really it isn't. The basin is small and only parts of my body will be in the basin at any one time. It is not a graceful sort of bathing and I am happier to be alone. There is too much gaping involved, gaping parts and a sort of tepid quality, which is not going to provide a feeling of clean. This has gotten to be very routine. Which at first it was not. Routine. I was scalding my oatmeal bowl and bread knife and my cleaning rags and my face towel but then it really became quite routine and now I don't think that much about germs or crumbs or bits of unidentified floating grease. It runs back to the body eventually. When you really begin to economize with something like water you see how cleanliness is a losing battle. It all wants to move toward crumbs and grease and loose hairs.

I need to have a bath and though the bathing becomes routine and uninteresting, it is something I try to keep up with. Particularly today. I am going to push away the crumbs and grease and loose hairs for just a while. I am going to be out tonight. This is not usual exactly, though occasionally I go to a place which is the closest place to go to but still pretty far. It is too far to walk, but it is not hard to find the way. A bar/restaurant. The bar/restaurant is almost like being on a boat or on something that has been made to seem like a boat. The illusion is incomplete, it is not in earnest, and this is actually a relief to me. It does not require that I believe. Even for a moment. I am completely comfortable with my disbelief in this place and its boatness or nauticality. It is warm and filled with spongy furniture. A kind of spool furniture and part of the imitative, non-boatness of it is a deck that butts onto a little harbor. In the harbor is a large ship and this ship is open to the public. Families in sweat suits are often walking to and fro on a little wooden bridge that leads to the deck of the large ship. It, too, is pretty unconvincing.

The bath is only partially satisfying. There is a point after which bathing will only make me feel less clean. This point arrives and I lift out of the basin. The day is very warm and I dry myself in the sun because the bathing towels are not clean themselves, being subject to these poor sanitizing conditions.

You might say that I should make a bit more of an effort. I've been there before. All the scenarios. Different methods of heating or containers or going down to the beach or distilling and I've run through these and it is all exhausting.

73

I think that I may be in the middle of a conversion experience, feeling a bit broken down. This is likely on account of making an effort against the forces of unidentifiable grease, floating things which defy categorization. It depresses me. Everything touching. It is a feeling I must shake. I must not convert quite yet. Perhaps when I am in the imitation-nautical bar, when I am drinking with the possibility of many drinks, then I can go over. For a while. I dress and put it all out of my mind and dream about sitting on the harbor and ordering a big basket of fried clams and potatoes. I must not think *hurricane* but *clams* and *cocktail sauce*.

I get a ride into the town with a teenage girl. She is large and has many huge bug bites on her neck and arms. She sees me staring at the welts and says, nervously, "I work outside." I smile at her. She looks confused. Like she is in someone else's clothes. She works outside she says and gets chewed up by bugs. *Perhaps day and night* I think. She is pleading. She is a look of pleading.

She is a thorn in my side.

She lives with a boy, she adds quickly, and they have a very nice place with sheer curtains. Then she says that she likes to sew and makes lots of clothes for her friends. She talks about patterns, fabrics, her golden retriever Bowser, and buttonholing. She is on her way to a large sewing store she says. It is open late and this is good because she works long hours. She has to, she says, because her boyfriend can't be a fisherman. He is missing parts. Of himself. She asks me what I am doing and I say that I am thinking about ordering up a big basket of fried clams. She is moist and trembling in the huge car.

"This is my mum's car," she says, a little embarrassed.

"It is all messages," I tell her. She says it uses a lot of gas and is expensive but using mum's car is the only way around things.

"Exactly," I say.

"A large fried clams and chips," I say. The bartender writes this down and swings back through the doors to the greasy little kitchen. I take my beer and some napkins and forks out to the deck on the harbor. Is sticky. The air. The table. The short beer glass. This is reassuring. The pub has already descended into a homeostatic filth and so there goes the business of working against that. I find that restful and drink this small beer. I am free to float a bit and then eat the fried clams and have all this greasy stickiness around me and inside me too. The pub is fully non-nautical and reassuring in its filth. The bartender's apron is dirty with chicken grease, beer stains, and the floor tar. Nothing can get much less clean. This place is in a continuous downhill. The bartender brings out my fried clams and I say, "This is just perfect," and he says nothing.

The radio is on announcing a small-plane accident offshore. The man says that there is no way yet to know what happened. It is likely that the man is dead because you can only live so long in ocean water. A small plane piloted by J.F.K. Jr., and many people call in speculating on how the plane went down. People say it is a curse. On the Kennedys. "Poor Caroline," they say. They still think of her as a cute little girl with a pony.

Hurricane.

I take out my notebook. For language retrieval. Back to the wreck. To the disaster. How did we talk then? Now it feels like language of a radio announcer or auction house. Like we used those words. *Going once. Going twice.* I feel a little guilty because it is possible that I have made the whole thing up. By thing, I mean you. I make you up. At the same time, I have not broken with reality. I know where you are. Or are not. You are not around. Even in dreams. I feel like I may have misrepresented some things. Like how lonely I am. Wanting to appear more in control. More like a guide to real places. Or having you be a heroine when really I want to bring you down.

Tear you down like a house.

Rolling house-world. You touch it. It crumbles.

That's not right either. Exactly. I mean we were both in a disaster. But the way they talked about you, you were a saint. Sweet. Happy. Planning birthday parties, color schemes, and bake sales. That is how everybody talked about you. "She was a saint," they said.

I remember you looking at me while he was trembling, angry. Shaking like he would shake me. He threw something at my head that seemed to explode. I have decided it was a lamp. He said, "You goddamn whore," and something exploded by my head. Or inside it. You only looked and shook your head no. You were saying that you would not interfere. You would not help me. You were saying *I am sorry but what can I do?* You were saying *I can't.*

He was in the hospital once. Do you remember that? You left in the ambulance with him and Cathy and I cried in our Great-Aunt Margaret's room. She patted my back saying, "bobish, bobish, bobish." That might have been Gaelic for something very soothing. We cried but she said, "Mommy will come back. She always does." Partly she was right. You did come back. And then we were alone, the three of us. You made things for dinner which were not usually allowed. Like pancakes and everything with catsup. Lots of sauce and gravy and butter with everything touching everything else. Exactly like he didn't like it. We were eating something on small plates and you sat where he normally sat and we sat closer.

It was just after Christmas and cold. We went with neighbors to skate on the small pond by the plant nursery. There were lots of unused Christmas trees stacked in front of the nursery doors. Inside, ornaments were on sale. Basketfuls. Cathy and I picked out two yarn-ball ornaments. Mine was a tiny snowman with a green hat and scarf. Cathy's was a brown dog with an orange and yellow striped cap. We bought them for you to bring to him in the hospital. I didn't want him to be lonely, but I didn't want him to come back either. I thought that they were nice presents. We spent a long time choosing and didn't fight. You brought them with you to the hospital. It was hard to see you leave. To believe you would come back from the hospital. It seemed like you went every day. But it was only for a few hours. Even then I knew it was unlikely that you would give him up altogether, all at once, so you going for a few hours was a compromise. You were going. You went but then you came home. I have to say, though, that I never quite trusted you to keep any sort of bargain. To keep us alone. Away from disaster. You were, I could see, a goner for disaster. You said, "It isn't so bad." Or "Don't overreact." Or "Why do you girls have to fight? You know all I ever wanted was a sister. I prayed for one. And all you two do is fight. One day I am going to be sick of your fighting. One day all of you will be sorry." But while he was in the hospital we didn't fight. Or at least not much. Even in the absence of disaster life is not perfect.

It was maybe a week before he came home. He was healed. He was strong as ever. You beamed, "Isn't this great?" Or maybe you were saying you had made a choice.

Last night Jeff said, "She had a nice laugh, didn't she?" And I said, "How did you know?"

hi I am not sure if you will get this but I went out

from Montreal today to the place your mother called God forsaken which I had always

misinterpreted as "Vietnam" but really she had meant "country"

as in "that God-forsaken country" terrible bumpy on the train

I start like this, they ask, "you got Canadian?"

and he then, "I got Keith's and Coors and Alpine" all night "I got Keith's and Coors
  and Alpine" I

have a head cold and then they say something about "my wife would pull it all in and I

like my wife you know and then sometimes . . . " it is a bit homey out

here am wanting home and easier but I am not Canadian

the baby says, "bye car," last night the conductor went through and the old drunk
  always

back there said, "isn't this grand and all we need is a bit of music on this train!"

and the guy said, "so sing it your own self," and there was a sad sort of singing
  through the country

and bye car bye-bye car and now I see my grandmother had meant God-forsaken
  country

meaning the fields the land and to me this was interpreted as being remembered
  in prayers I

had a little packet of jam on my toast today a toy dropped into the center aisle of
  the train

it appeared to be eating a plush carrot and there seemed to be farms for sale
  passing out-

side in St. Rosalie or a soybean canning factory bye car and the elaborate pitch of a
    woman always
speaking French, the wheezy laughing and "you got Canadian?"

today the train pushes northeast, harder into the Canadian
country in a slow movement opposing the direction my grandmother took to leave
    the country
where near everything had died, the countless siblings born dead or dying "always
someone was dying," she said and about the not high-flown enough demeanor of
    someone I
suppose she meant that they were all dirt farmers she wanted out
and then had a house in Queens with linoleum and a plastic train

laid across the living room carpet which you were not supposed to step off on the train
today a young girl in a stocking cap and soft arms is reading *On the Road* thinking
    of it as Canadian
I remember reading that being, I think, nineteen and desperate to get out of New
    York City just out
last night I dreamt someone asked "what do you make of this poem?" but it was a
    foreign country
and the question came across as what does it mean if I
paste this "face-of-a-poet" sticker on to my own photograph noting that yes, this
    was me always

a bit thinner or drinking much more heavily and in the dream it always
takes much longer to conjure up the faces, to fasten, in the dream (asleep on the train)
all the little boys' heads which are lighter and snowy and cleaner than any real
    person could be I
woke up (bye car) noticing the signs why are so many Canadian

houses scheduled for demolition? in tunnels my reflection is suddenly in place of
     the country
I am darker and it startles me because I have recently become some sort of
     brunette out

there is just me but always darker on the route you must have taken for summers
     up here
and you watched all this country go by the train it just passes and I overhear bits of
     conversation
Canadians like the young mother of two or bye car bye-bye car but I am not really
     in any of it, ever

hi again I am still trying to remember this story of an event in time

the time was one day after you died and it is too bad because it was just getting good

I mean the story, it takes a giant leap forward into melodrama around then we had
    taken

a cab from La Guardia and arrived at the house which was really very silent

I began to have an experience without understanding the surface but was suddenly

engulfed, wanting to retrieve your wedding ring from the coroner I thought this
    listening to the radio

as a means of addressing myself as witness to the event we were listening to the radio

playing those kind of top 40 songs that I really hated at that time

those songs made me want to kill myself back then something like *Little Pink*
    Houses could suddenly

make me want to kill myself but instead I was thinking how I would have to come
    up with a good

plan to get the wedding ring back from the coroner and we were silent

in the cab the driver asking questions just trying to be nice like what flight had
    we taken

or were we brother and sister and stuff like that and we said it was a red-eye flight
    we had taken

the driver said that it was really nice, warm weather and where had we come from,
    adjusting the radio

he must have said things like that but I was unable to witness the event beginning
    this silent

repetition of the experience I say these are the facts because it must have happened
    that way in time
to have us end up at the house because people just don't magically get from an
    airport a good
distance away to a house maybe the song or the wedding ring was living testimony
    to us suddenly

passing innumerable times from the airport to the house but in any event we were
    suddenly
at the house, or more precisely in the driveway and the first thing I remember for
    real is being taken
into the arms of a priest and it is still silent but in this part I see that the day is good
and warm and I see this in spite of being engulfed in the embrace of the priest
    the radio
is silent, my brother is silent or speaking very, very softly and this time
I speak and I say I would like to get the wedding ring but they act as if I am silent

and those little nothing questions like *isn't it a nice day* are almost heartbreaking I
    am silent
not humming along or anything and not reliable enough to render true histories
    suddenly
looking at the sky (it was a beautiful day) and the mothball smell of the priest's
    clothes, this time
I see the sky reminding me I am part of what human life does like wearing
    nightgowns or being taken
from an airport to a house (you missed that part) or being seduced by a voice on
    the radio
and it pretty much went like that the work engaged with each use of the body I
    guess a good

way to spend time I went inside and either Dean was there or came in just after me
   which was good
because I asked him, "can you get the ring for me?" and he heard that part, I
   wasn't exactly silent
in the kitchen someone said, "is there enough decorative icing to go around?" and
   the clock radio
on the counter still tuned to your favorite songs, it was a Sinatra-a-thon then
   suddenly
Dean is there again and he hands me the ring and this has happened very quickly
   the ring was taken
from your body or at least the bit that was left of it and I turn the band over and
   over, this time

looking for blood or some evidence of burning not just the body implied passed
   time it is no good
there is no you anywhere I am taken between the event and the ring which is
   silent, a monument
suddenly in memorial, women were making cakes—giant birthday-like cakes—
   listening to the radio

how do you know God wants you to win?
because you have won, of course sometimes you have to go to the great sign
readers, like Cromwell was a great sign reader he saw that England has this problem
it did not yet own Europe and certain effects are done and undone in a poem
others have a diminishing vocabulary like to only write of gardens would say
something because there are a lot of flower names and then the Latin one

which can become musical after so much English one
way to break up all the English the way Milton could win
out in the end after he saw painting and Michelangelo so say
I could narrow my vocabulary work away from the signified to the sign
as in not mentioning the body in the poem
but only what the body laid out read as a sign but there is a problem

because there was no body, no signified substance a problem
identified as "the car exploded shortly upon impact" one
person pulled from the wreck and one not so that in the poem
the body which had meant some things like growing, the chance to win
or in some sense love ceased to be and so the sign
those things it had meant it could no longer continue to say

standing at the kitchen sink the water always running, could not say
"listen this is the best part" (she turned the radio up) or "what *is* your problem?"
(I had so many) her hand moving around the pans like a sign
often eating a bit of chicken cleaning she ate more at the sink than at the table one

last bite "because it came out pretty good, didn't it?" how could we win?
how could I have asked her *why are we here,* in this house, or in this poem

why do we all have to stay under? his walking upstairs complicates the poem
because once again, it could never just be about us she would stop and say
"I have to get these dishes done," pop chicken bones into the trash win
"what?" she might have asked when she was a real body, as in *what is your problem?*
so did she know how we lived knocked us down, the one
time she said "I would never have believed that it would be like this," was that a sign?

I was determined not to miss it, if it came, the sign
that she was with me but who knows if it came, if it is embedded in the poem
she had a beautiful turquoise ring that we have never seen since then the one
that had cracked but still was beautiful she was beautiful I would say
now because I have looked at many pictures and that is how they look the problem
is if you look away you miss the sign or if you look at something too long, you just
    can't win

there was no way to win it was 4 A.M. and the knock at the door was a sign
(the one in this poem) my brother stood there (thousand miles from his home)
    there was a problem
he started to say "there has been an accident" my mother, once again, had not been
    the lucky one

THE SUN IS IN ARIES AND THE MOON IS GOING FROM
TAURUS INTO GEMINI. BE A GOOD LISTENER, BUT DON'T SAY
MUCH. YOUR BOSS MAY DECIDE TO UNLOAD. DON'T LET THE
INFORMATION YOU GATHER BE A BURDEN. INSTEAD, USE IT
TO ADVANCE YOUR MUTUAL CAUSE. THE MORE YOU CAN BE
TRUSTED, THE GREATER YOUR INFLUENCE GROWS.

I have been reading a lot since you died, reading a lot since you can be a burden
in a cafe in Lâ Have a woman asked, "do you know anything about bikes?" I
    was reading
about chaos theory, (she on her first bike trip at forty-five) chaos theory and/or
    Bernadette Mayer poems
and/or there was something gone wrong and/or Bernadette Mayer poems, gather
I was no use, but there it is—bikes and chaos all I do anyway is read and in 1991 I
    advanced
to reading interviews with famous French feminists and suddenly realized I didn't
    want a compact

washer/dryer and/or anything from Kustard King ruining the social compact
of who should ask who to bear the burden
of finding a Kustard King at three in the morning, advanced
example of the needy one exchanging places with the needy or reading
Anna Karenina and writing *we have been eating every two hours* gather
that meant something to me then or I thought it might later go into poems

which were still, generally, a little world all to myself, a lot of really bad poems
out of control of the so-much-more-out-of-control material, a compact
notation system, in which I made lists (1–24) I gather
that number 20, *murky*, had nothing to do with number 19, *lips, fuzzy*, a burden

trained to note-take in secrecy, one day I was reading

Walter Benjamin, "To articulate the past historically does not mean to recognize

(or advance)

'the way it really was' to seize hold of a memory as it flashes up at a moment of

danger." an advance

I think you might appreciate now, that as a moment of danger, in my poem,

the more you died the less scary it could become as if indeed number 13 went on

reading:

nice cows, look like cut-outs the handbag too charred to decipher your initials

on the compact

N.W. you don't say much but I want to read all of this for you, too—the burden

of having to do all the reading and/or talking now, I gather

you realize I do all the talking but that day I was reading, a woman asked, "do

you gather

up reading material," curious entertainment (I read on a very advanced

level) the woman was afraid of bike accidents but then one had occurred, the burden

off of *maybe* and onto *flat tire* she had a gash on her face, I had some poems

I was gone wrong, no use, but there it is, an idea: bikes and something compact

the tiny air pump "I don't know how it works" I said continuing with my reading

"what about me?" I said "do you know what it is like to be reading

for two people? all the possible books?" today I have no guidance, I gather

them randomly: the *Oxford Dictionary of Quotations* is up top, a compact

listing of all your favorites, perhaps the *Hélène Cixous Reader*? you feared the

politically advanced

and preferred to speak through fashion magazines "Runway's New Red Mouth,"
   or rhyming poems
you tell me, you know, for once, you tell me, I realize, you died but it's getting to be
   a burden

your not reading is a fucking burden confused about whether my horoscope means
   something for me
or you (same birth sign), if I wrote in poems *you can't help but like it* meaning you
   or me gather
all of what we have read, I have advanced us, I try, I honor that compact

faced each other across the piano we had taken piano lessons together but stopped
and faced off each other across what was suddenly loosened, her flushed cheeks
    this struggle
was sex and a preoccupation with sex
and me, I was moving, my virginity loosened like an overly simplistic metaphor except
that it was less Darwinian or maybe just less about survival a flavorless no-man's-
    land we undefined
it as me and the familiar/usual relationship previously obedient

we faced each other across the familiar safeguarding, suggesting an obedient
style of dress to avoid but her extraordinary indifference was lazy it stopped
me, "you're not sleeping with him, are you?" quickly defined
my answer, "no" but thinking *who* my virginity had not held had introduced
    the struggle
into a new way we faced each other all the other times I was a child except
this unmistakable dimension when I was battled in with sex

and me because for whatever it was worth I was having sex
just as the nonperformance of nonsensical profanities might have signaled I was
    less obedient
but not to anything said, more to a vein of inquiry or familiar blush except
we used childlike wonder for unlanguaging terror a way to focus that extraordinary
    focus stopped
and I continued to have sex and she continued to not have it the struggle
or failure to perform might have meant jealousy I am unable to remember, slowly
    she was defined

as a way to avoid having sex or a way not to feel it, I defined

her that way though I did continue to have sex

rolling his car noiselessly from the school grounds to get somewhere where we
    could struggle

turtlenecks and my own giant overalls I was obedient

in that I did not fail to feel guilty and that was all that she had asked, "you're
    not . . . " and stopped

she said once that it was nice but that meant except

if you are not married and this is to be regarded as something firm except

she seemed lazy about it posed in relation to "well your grandmother never liked
    it" she defined

it often, "some things have to be done but then there is gardening" "they stopped,"

my mother said of her own parents, "after me" "Hollywood," my grandmother
    said, "is about sex"

that was hard to argue against but I didn't feel very "Hollywood" more disheveled
    and disobedient

as we faced each other across the familiar being loosened in romantic love it was
    my struggle

to be in love because that was almost as good as marriage the struggle

I have not quite abandoned that no-man's-land half-Hollywood half-flat-chested
    adolescence except

maybe to parody a more self-satisfied self, the one with fewer problems obedient

untroubled person of sportswear catalogues, you know, we are still facing, defined

like chaining generations the way we came tightly to be here is so obviously sex

still safeguarding it in safety, I mean there are some funny jobs in this world if
    you stopped

to think about it? stopped to think about how to struggle, find something

with each other? we never used the word *sex* except, maybe, when it was defined

by "we have

touched on an unpleasant subject" I had taken it from her, backstabbing, not

exactly obedient

September is ringed this way: a mistake
made hopeless tiny hopeless days which lead to the one imaginary
day the day we agree should not have been added in loss of your identity, your
personality opens
and a High Mass provided ample opportunity for someone to whisper
"she was such a happy person" every person could repeat that in sick religion
we started this story almost immediately, the smoke still smoking gold ringing
September

car crash, a location appropriate just normal September
seen lots of those, the last person to see you alive pays his check perhaps makes
a mistake
calculating just how much a turkey sandwich costs, religion
prevents us from eating all the available meats imaginary
failure to express myself emotionally, so how it was a whisper
"she was such a happy person" and if you think that is funny it opens

with "she was so calm" and you should have seen the Jell-O salads fridge opens
and it is filled with Jell-O salad, every color, what seems like September
is nothing more than the human digestive system I whisper
(I am no longer speaking in a normal voice ever), "there is some mistake
we don't eat Jell-O salad," but who can believe my imaginary
version of you from Flushing just another part of Queens where you kept religion

separate because it was obvious that religion
was not terribly sophisticated, but there it was, finally, you had a High Mass opens

with the eulogy (happy, calm) we covered that part but the fact is Cathy is not there,
  just imaginary
mostly to me because I am there she is in the hospital for the rest of September
I keep forgetting to walk the dog and sleep until someone gives me a Haldol
  obviously a mistake
because then I make profiteroles, lasagne, bean soup and still am not sleeping
  whisper

"I am not sleeping anymore," but lay down so that others won't grow concerned and
  whisper
"she was such a happy, calm person" whispering *is* calming I used the words
  like *religion*
treacherous to account for the presence of tragedy, it was hard work not to mistake
the way we called one thing *calm* and another *treacherous* finally it opens
out into another month beginning right on schedule and this did surprise me,
  September
completing itself like that her nylon nightdress seemed imaginary

still in a basket by the stairs I would have washed clothes for the imaginary
you, the imaginary mother who continued out into the frost morning a long whisper
of a nightgown with a fitted blazer thrown over to happily, calmly approach September
morning newspaper of tragedy a religion
of daily tragedy I later dreamt you were Cybill Shepherd but still outside in that
  outfit, he opens
the paper, you never read it saying, "look I don't even have time to read the paper it
  is a mistake

for me to even try" a mistake to take anything too seriously—the imaginary
life of not cooking and cleaning or other irresistible behavior opens breathing
   whisper but what
did matter? religion contended? space shuttle disaster? what outrageous hope for
   that September?

the hundred or so dumb help prepare giant platters of cold cuts without losing
a moment in setting out trays of tiny cut-up cakes old
dishes I have not seen in years overripe fruit is so sad
and deflating in odd ashtrays or any number of strange crockeries it
is a round of hazelnuts or mini-quiche nothing
less appropriate at all times than the mini-quiche or odd gourd

stuffed with something like limp salad using the poor gourd
as some sort of punch bowl or roundup losing
its shape and orangeness, chilling ring of Jell-O salad nothing
conspires with a funeral like Jell-O salad it is the good old
standard of the this-and-thatness, dull animal vanity they said, "it
is absolutely tragic, just like Grace Kelly," I make attempts at grooming but made
    a sad

crooked braid (being so right-dominant) I guess the hair in my face didn't reveal as
    much sad
or else there was some concern about the food preparation—no one wants a gourd
full of hair, the outskirts of summer ringing September all fruit, well, it
is a way of conspiring, that we were all losing
her was most apparent in the kind of food she would never have prepared or old
vases holding Triskets, *over my dead body*, she would have said *nothing*

doing, I didn't become middle-class for this nothing
in the way of how she could be disciplined, all that out, the hundred dumb
    perceptions sad

that the leaves began to collect along the base of trees and old

lamppost resting against that lamppost where she had rested pumpkins, a gourd

an attempt to communicate from the beyond to our hundred dumb losing

sight of how she had kept it colorful and fresh (counters always clean) it

became hidden—how she had kept it

all—ripe fruit rolled to the window sill, close-blossomed hydrangea rotting nothing

getting any fresher, but still laid out so many sweating cheeses, apples, and quinces
     losing

their pale meat browning all around our hundred sad

and various nut shells husks tucked into planters or behind the autumn gourd

arrangements I had no dress to wear so instead wore an old

one of hers not the Halston or chiffon but an old

navy blue with tiny white strawberry blossoms it

was hot like a hangover inside the house, buzzing with a hundred flies around
     the gourd

fruit arrangement "crickets sing all the time now," I said to the toothpick garnish,
     feeling nothing

high on Haldol, the dress didn't fit well and made a sad

sort of spectacle with crooked hair—I had the idea to try to do everything but felt I
     was losing

that fight, losing all the best parts, days could not cease slow-dying and old

garden fruit gummy sad and hundreds of people seemed to say it say "is there

nothing we could do?" while casually dropping a gourd, jelly-like, in the sweet,
     close smell of trash

HAS ANYONE CONSIDERED THE POSSIBILITY THAT IT WAS A SUICIDE?

she was deep into certain passages certain
making her way along the planks clumsy and not downed yet but captured
"fuck this" she may have said her face the angry clover full-
figured for the first time because menopause works that way
or "is it hot in here? is it just me?" she reprised this role, moving
from disaster to disaster and if you liked her in (blank) you'll love

her in (blank) always a hit, studious outthrust of her rounder self the love
all around her, how could you not love someone who is certain
to be the first to admit it? the last one to know oh-a-oh-oh saying, "it must be me,"
    moving
through the pathetic holding of such pet thoughts captured
kind of deer-in-headlights face choosing a chorus of we can try harder to do it his way
she sang for several weeks in each location, once she had inspired proposals but
    now full

of plans for the new kitchen, happy only then creating the one which would make
    her full
and not miss the heavy melodrama of losing someone to love
because I had plans to be in the class of 1989, Great Literature, moving
out there in America and she was (worst of all) captured
I would not be back to the new kitchen busy throwing away all the wish for
    gentility, certain
there was no going home again after Great Literature and the way

my mother asked, "Alice Cooper, who's she?" or the way
I had started to suspect that she liked it the fat, full
way the house had boiled and boiled all of us captured
by something there was no way to identify in a line-up, confused love
was somehow equal to fighting very stubbornly for the sense of existence certain
that the fighting never made a difference it didn't work that way

over sandwiches thickly I had the thought that she had wanted it this way
the confinement, the absence of her own checking account, never moving
never walking out even when weeks where crafty ruined because a certain
phone message was inexact, nothing was small or good or possible enough
    the house full
of potential interruption by "are you stupid?" it must have been something she
    could love
I thought and bewildered I meant to slide out, carefully escaping capture

and the brave swagger of "what are you, an idiot?" but of course, capture
is not in the street or the bed or the eating sandwiches it came the way
everything comes, screaming, hot and heavy footed, came in the face of what I love
most it came in the body casual as my own, moving
toward me with her steady way of explaining and apologizing all at once full
and glutted with every joke she had told improperly or chicken she had been certain

was too dry certain it was too tough, captured
in that gesture which went something like a full minute of holding her figure that way
she crashed in a car and inside her body was still moving, that body unfortunately
    came to equal love

PART THREE

I.

when I look up western civilization

it begins when
I place the small plastic teapot
picked up at age three on an imaginary stove
are all stoves pink?
is this part hot?
pink gingham brought on anxiety
my anxiety about losing
about
can I write
can I shell the absence of
you looked like the source of my anxiety
trembling when I split my chin
I had to calm you down
about me
companionship had its source
in the absence of human companionship
not is need
because I did not so much
like when you said, "it's not so bad."

II.

the hand all around

in

hand always looking

slept some nights in an itchy sweater

just wanted to keep the *out* out

when is the mountain a cone?

in the Grand Canyon

I have your you when I feel red

I have you I have you and me

us out

lightning is the only light

on my body

things the lightning touches barely

on my birthday you make a cake

but something happens and you have to throw it away

and by something I mean

you know what I mean

there are the we places

like that birthday

when I was awake all night altered

wracked with sobbing

just like a person in a book about something bad happening

and you distant but drawn-out, "it is not so bad."

then years later I heard

that you saw that cake in the trash

and lay down on the floor crying

saying,

"don't go"

III.

I'm the only one perceivable now
nocturnal
doing things the living do

are these walls?

my t-shirt on sheets
seems one sound
the
the body difficult
night cars passing I dream
I'm birds,
etc. having a birthday
but in the dream birthdays are mountains
and they are also cones
I have another dream
I am walking outside at a ski resort past where one returns the skis
plywood shelves
I pass a series of these shelves and inside
there are Christmas trees wrapped up in sheets
with all of their decorations
cones or more cocoon
I need to choose one but can't
they seem
skin cones or seem alien
snow, etc. falls from a height but

the white is

really gulls which pass, etc.

I write *berf-day* in the snow

with small motor parts

IV.

I cannot stop moving

I am moving again

I make a list of things I want in life:

    lettuce

    eye wash (which I write as ice wash but later correct)

    itch cream

    mayo

later I recognize these things as groceries

I feel fidgety

I should be doing things but bricked-up

ticking off numbers

and waiting for you

am I hanging you up yet?

V.

we went to the movies and saw a film in French
about a woman who could not accept the death of her husband
after he disappeared mysteriously at the beach
even when a body was found in the sea
even when presented with his most intimate possessions
she could not
accept it
she found out many things about her husband when he disappeared
he had lived a secretive life
or at least there were some secrets
like he was depressed and on medication
she had not known that
her mother-in-law claims that her son is not dead
that he has disappeared to get away from his wife
whom the mother had never liked
the mother reveals this and the wife is
demolished
she fears it to be true
and begins to imagine that her husband
is alive and living in their apartment
but then his watch is found in the ocean
near the spot where he was last seen
and all along the wife is teaching a class on Virginia Woolf
where she reads aloud from *The Waves*

by the end you are pretty sure he really is dead

but the wife is running toward something on the beach

she is running like she sees him

VI.

I am hiking to the ocean past Drake's Bay
scrubby bluff up to ridge top it is so open it is like
walking on a map

Proust said:
"the past is somewhere beyond the reach of intellect and unmistakably present in
some material object."

I have to map
to placate
to know where to place
in an agitated list of locate
I am isolated in looking
I look here on the fog-socked land
out to the ocean or up close
to a path by
scrub pine
believing I'll find you
everywhere
here or in a castle in the Portuguese forest
where I heard a woman's voice speaking English
or sitting at a restaurant in New York City

VII.

sitting in a restaurant in New York City

you come in

take a seat

there is the smallest sound of your shoes

touching as your ankles cross

you have a companion

you are well dressed and rested

wearing reading glasses you regard the elegant menu

in a kind of inattention of your surroundings

you breathe out audibly

you "hmm . . . "

and I look over

I notice you first, your hand

the way you cock your thumb in and out

it is an identifying tic

VIII.

you are hungry and want to order right away
you look up in a gesture that is youthful
girlish
terrifying

IX.

I am surprised and proud

because I looked for so long

I catch your eye and

say, "I have read Proust, Woolf, Derrida, Barthes, Hawthorne, Keats, O'Neill,

Acker, Cather, Hegel—everything."

I say, "if I did everything,

I knew I would find you

even though I saw your purse charred by explosion

and the car and Cathy was hurt for a long time

but is better now."

and then I say, "I knew"

but you look through me

toward the waiter and begin ordering

"a salad to start and what is the *confit?*"

I interrupt, a little frantically, "remember me?"

I say and I try to think of something

which might remind you of me

but realize that there is nothing

I have

phantom evidence that I was there

you are far away like Zola or Neptune's moons

the moment rotates

in a slow-motion sort of way

I can't believe it and

want to continue

trying, etc. but am panicking

I tell you I am taking pills for

this panicking but really want to say

can't you just

try

you just don't see me

you don't look

or I look so different

or maybe you are saying

X.

so it continues choosing, unchoosing
so many times I can't write them all
far out there
so away as to remain,
temporarily, unseen
but today, right here,
ordering this salad
thinking "screw the no-wheat diet,
I will have the *confit* over pasta"
a flame-flash
we eclipse perfectly

It started somewhere. In a place where there were visible manifestations of cruelty on a daily basis. She said things which were unkind. It was thrilling. She blamed it on menopause. She was reading novels in tawny jackets. Thrillers. Romances. She would be in a conversation, lose interest, then pick up the novel which had been turned face down on the carpet beside her. It was the first time she did this that it seemed most rebellious. To not listen. To not wear a face of concern. To not remain there. To take this action of being apart from people for the first time in her life. She read novels rapidly and in a rage. Feverish only in her hands.

She said, "I forget things." And, "I think it is hormonal." But she did not put aside the books. There was a stillness all around her, but she was whirring. This was determined to be the sense of destruction left in the wake of her turning away.

She looked over her reading glasses at him and said, "If someone had told me, fifteen years ago, that we would end up like this, I never would have believed them." It wasn't what she said but the fact that she was no longer pleading. It was a message.

She is driving. She drives and drives, never looking at the gas gauge. She thinks that the temperature gauge is really the gas gauge and is shocked when the car runs out of gas. "I could have sworn," she says, returning home in a taxi. She learns to read the gas gauge and goes out driving. Again she tells no one where she is going. *Driving is like reading novels*, she thinks, *because I am alone.*

Then she is home again and sunny. She wants to do lots of ironing. She irons things which had been in the ironing bag for years. She finds two new blouses this way. Even though they are old. Some days she forgets about the novels and driving and says things to him like, "Do I look fat in this?" And he says, "What do you want me to say?" and he is relieved to hear a kind of pleading. But she continues to eat. She eats half a chicken while washing the dishes after dinner. She does this systematically, stripping each tiny, greasy bone. Leftover rice pilaf makes her inexplicably sad and she throws it away. He is enraged at this new wastefulness, but she does it anyway. She asks, "Is it hot in here?"

She cries in front of the mirror. She pinches the purse of skin under her chin. She still stands pushing the heel of her left foot into the arch of her right, but now she thinks of this posture as slimming.

She examines me and says, "You can't wait to leave, can you? You can't wait to leave me." I say that is not true but that I have to leave. "You know I have to leave," I say. "But you could be sad," she says. I say nothing. I am sitting on the stairs and she is ironing. She says, "Well, I guess you are happy to be leaving. Only two weeks and you'll be free of us. I guess you are happy." "It isn't so far away," I say. "Yeah, it is," she says. "I have to go sometime," I say. "But you could be sad about it. You won't even miss me," she says.

I don't know what to say. There is a glass of lemonade resting on one end of the ironing board. It shakes with the rubbing of the iron and the ice makes a small bell sound. "Ma," I say.

I make x's on the days left until I leave, and then the day arrives and I go. The trail of x's follow me. I am all x's and nots. I will not ever have to do x. I can go to the pharmacy and just look at stuff for as long as x. I can eat x. I can talk about x. I can fall asleep without thinking what happens after x. I can stop eating all the time to keep from saying x. I can stop reading into x. I can buy frivolous food for dinner like x. I can stop worrying.

But I don't. She sends me a letter full of grammatical mistakes. I wonder if this is a message but have nothing to compare it to because she has never written anything to me before. She sends me brownies that Cathy has made for me. She sends me a small gray pillow. She writes that for a person who likes to talk so much, she is not a very good letter writer. She writes that she misses me "lots." I read this as a message which is translated to mean something about how we are drawn to disaster. I speak to her on the phone trying to be calm. I tell her that everything is fine, but I have no idea if this is true.

After a few weeks she visits me. She is not alone, but I can almost pretend she is. I am excited to see her and wait, sitting half in the open window, for her. I see her walking on the sidewalk outside the building where I live and I call out her name. She looks around and I say, "Up here." She looks up and looks so young, like a teenager. It is a youthful gesture as she turns to look up. "I found you," she laughs.

We have dinner and the next morning, in the hotel room, she is putting on her makeup and talking to me about all the people we know. I can see her most intimate moments: smoothing the skin, the skin of her clothes, the script of her, alone before a mirror smoothing a bit of pale, delicious ice-creamy cream over the apples of her cheeks. We are like this until she leaves and she is standing in the parking garage and he is waiting, impatient. She is standing there. She says, "I miss you so much." She says, "I don't want to go." I decide to laugh, to say, "Oh, c'mon. I'll see you soon. Cathy's birthday." And I continue efforts at standing. Nonchalance. "I feel like you are breaking," I want to say. I want to say, "It is treacherous." I want to say, "We have no sanctioned outlet for our grief." He revs the motor. She says things which will keep the truth at bay a few moments longer. She is breaking. I can't cry or touch her. It alludes too much to something absent. If only I had some sort of cheery accent. I try to think urgently about something like God or capitalism. The abundance of topics.

Do you remember Miss Matching Umbrella? Or the male flight attendants who lived next door and loved your outfits? How little Chubbs Carter crawled out the window of the A&P but was okay? Or how March is the hardest month to abbreviate?

He rolls down the window and yells for her to get in the car. "Enough's enough," he says. I say, "Well, I guess you better get going," and she turns back toward the car and says to him, "I'm going, I'm going."